William J. Potter

The National Tragedy

four sermons delivered before the First Congregational Society, New

Bedford, on the life and death of Abraham Lincoln

William J. Potter

The National Tragedy
four sermons delivered before the First Congregational Society, New Bedford, on the life and death of Abraham Lincoln

ISBN/EAN: 9783337087340

Printed in Europe, USA, Canada, Australia, Japan

Cover: Foto ©ninafisch / pixelio.de

More available books at **www.hansebooks.com**

THE NATIONAL TRAGEDY:

FOUR SERMONS

DELIVERED BEFORE THE

FIRST CONGREGATIONAL SOCIETY, NEW BEDFORD,

ON THE LIFE AND DEATH

OF

ABRAHAM LINCOLN.

BY WILLIAM J. POTTER.

New Bedford, Mass.:
ABRAHAM TABER & BROTHER.
1865.

PRINTED BY REQUEST.

———————

NEW BEDFORD:

I.

THE ASSASSINATION OF THE PRESIDENT.

——————~~~~~~~~~~——————

We looked for peace, but no good came; and for a time of health, and behold, trouble! Jer. viii. 15.

Their sword shall enter into their own heart. Ps. xxxvii. 15.

MY FRIENDS, how can I fitly speak to you to-day? How can any human words lift the burden from our hearts? How can any human wisdom fathom the Providence of this national tragedy under whose awful shadow we come together? Our staggered faith asks, indeed, if there be any Providence in this foul deed; and reason and reverence and piety, all that is most cogent in truth and all that is most holy in religion, cry out,—No! there *is* no Providence in it! No Providence save that which belongs to the blackest crime,—no Providence save that which permits the foulest cruelty to wreak its demoniac spirit on unoffending innocence, and does not, by miraculous interposition, stay the stealthy assassin's blow,—no Providence save that which always surrounds the dreadful fact of sin, and by which sin is made, in its last desperate madness, to overleap all bounds, even of its own appointing, and to bring down upon itself, in its own destruction, all the

righteous indignation and vengeance of Heaven's justice!
It were blasphemy to speak of any other Providence than
this in the dark, midnight crime that has slain our President.
It is the hand of Satanic wickedness that has done this
thing; and the hand of the Lord is not in it, save as it
enters into every crime, to neutralize, overturn, and destroy
it, result and cause together.

I pray not—I dare not pray—for meek submission,
as if this were God's act. I pray rather for a just
indignation, for a wise and righteous wrath to inspire us,—
not for any littleness of vindictive passion, not for any
spirit of human vengeance,—but with reverent earnestness
and solemn sense of the hour's need, I pray that the mighty
spirit of Heaven's retributive justice may possess and stir
our hearts, and put into us the iron nerve that is wanted for
the stern tasks now given to our hands. I pray, indeed,
that thy will, O Lord, not ours, may be done,—but it is not
thy will to slay the beauty of Israel on our high places,—it
is the unsanctified, maddened, wicked will of man that has
done this deed, thinking, in its insensate frenzy, to fight
against and overthrow thy will. Yea, O Lord, thy will be
done! Thus may we ever pray. And may we listen
reverently, docilely, courageously, to hear thy will even in
this fearful tragedy, with hearts and hands ready to do to
the utmost whatsoever duty is required of us. For, though
not by thy righteous will has this dreadful thing been done,
yet *in it* thou sendest us warning, and instruction, and great
commands. Let us listen and obey.

Listen for yourselves, O friends. I cannot hope, and I
have not the heart to attempt to-day, to interpret this

national calamity, and this crime against the nation, in their full significance. Our sense of loss is too personal,—it will not let us yet fully uncover the sacred reserve of our grief; it is yet too soon—we cannot bear—to have the curtain lifted wholly, and the fearful horror exposed in all its secret causes and consequences. But listen—listen each for himself—to what truth and justice and a wise, true love, are trying, through the passages of this grief, to utter to-day in every loyal heart. Listen, my friends, for God's voice, as he shall utter in your stirred and agonized souls the *moral* of this awful tragedy. Listen and obey.

The lesson must come. But I can only hint at it to-day. It is not yet the hour for analysis, but for grief.

For grief! Oh, double grief, that in the hour of our triumph this wickedness has been consummated! that into the hour of our rejoicing this heavy sadness falls! that the bells had hardly rung out their gladness through the land before they had to mournfully toll the people's sorrow! Double grief, that he who had led us so wisely, and with so much honor to himself and the country, through the terrors of war, has fallen by the assassin's hand, just as he was going through the gates of victory to receive the crown of peace and of a nation's gratitude! The crown of peace! He wears it now from God's own hands. The crown of a nation's gratitude! He is henceforth our martyr and our saint.

Grief not for him! But grief that our hands cannot bestow the crown which his have so nobly won, and that our eyes cannot see him wear it, moving with honors and grateful love among us down to serene old age. Double grief, that just as peace was dawning, and the whole east was radiant with the coming sun of prosperity and joy, the sky is suddenly darkened with the blackness of this guilt and this tempest of a nation's tears!

I thought to speak to you to-day, my friends, of the glory of Petersburg and Richmond; of the overthrow and surrender of the great army of the rebellion, and of the old flag raised again by brave Anderson's hands over Fort Sumter,— of the open door and auspicious harbingers of peace. But "we looked for peace, and behold trouble." We looked for peace, and behold a sword.

Four years ago this crime would not have shocked us as it does now. Then we almost expected it, and it was almost a miracle that it did not come. But now, after being saved through the hazards of four years of open war and stealthy treachery, that this precious blood should be spilled, by the dastardly assassin's hand, on the very threshold of final victory,— it is for this that our hearts weep and almost refuse to be comforted, and our shocked, staggering faith asks, "Why, O why, was this consecration, and this baptism needed, before we could enter again the holy temple of peace?"

We weep not for him. His career is finished gloriously. Few public men in this, or any, land will have so honorable a record in history. The people's president—not the president of politicians, or of a party, but the president of the people and the country,—coming from the people, respected, honored, trusted, beloved, chosen and re-chosen by the people, he aimed always with upright and manly purpose to serve the people, and advance their interests and their rights. The most magnanimous and tender-hearted and forgiving of magistrates, he has almost fallen a victim to his own generous nature. Standing in presence of the open grave which violence has prepared for him, we forget even the few faults of his character. His life rounds before us in majestic fulness and completion; and whether for the sober pen of the future historian, or for the dramatic demands of some coming Shakspeare, he could hardly have himself asked for a longer continuance of life. For him,—for his fame, for a sure place in his country's gratitude, for his immortality in history or in dramatic story, his life is finished with rare and æsthetic felicity. It received its crown when, a few days ago, he made that modest but triumphant entry into Richmond, hailed, not by the rich and the powerful, but by the poor blacks, whose chains by his command had just fallen from their limbs, and who crowded the way and followed him through the streets, showering their blessings upon him as their deliverer and saviour. That was the crown of his presidency and his life. After that there was no honor which the country or the world could give him. We weep not, then, for him. He is henceforth our hero as well as our martyr-president.

Nor do we mourn for our country's cause, as if that were lost. In thus completing and crowning his own life, he had conducted the nation to the point of assured triumph and safety. Not for our country's cause can we now grieve or fear. That, thanks to our dead president, thanks to our generals and their armies, thanks to the Lord of Hosts, is now beyond the power of any one man's life or death either to save or to destroy.

Not for our country's *cause* do we mourn ; but we do weep for our country's loss and dishonor. We weep for the State, bereaved of an honest, faithful, unselfish ruler. We weep for philanthropy, bereaved of a sagacious counsellor and helper. We weep for humanity, bereaved of the tenderest and most compassionate of hearts. We weep for the whole world of mankind, bereaved of a statesman who had faith, without regard to race, or color, or country, in the laws of divine justice, and in a government of equal rights and equal chances for all. But most of all do we weep for the enormity of this crime,— that the assassin, at home under despotism, but a stranger to our free government, has been permitted to put his brand of infamy upon the Republic, and to stain forever its hitherto fair escutcheon with more precious than imperial blood. Flow, tears of this people, till you wash out in expiation the "damned spot" of this guilt! Drop your tears in floods, O clouds, to cover our shame! Let the sun and the moon and the pure heavens be darkened, that they see not our sin! Oh, humanity, that thou couldst have borne this dreadful crime in thy bosom! In all the world there is but one that equals it. We must go back eighteen hundred years, to Gethsemane and Mount Calvary, to find its fitting mate in atrocity.

Yet not upon the skirts of the Republic, not upon the sceptre or royal robes of freedom, rests this stain. It is the exotic spirit of despotism that has committed this horror. Slavery has done this deed. Slavery, which has educated a whole community in barbarism, which has corrupted all sense of honor and right and truth in its upholders, which gave birth to the monstrous theory of secession, and fomented treason and conspiracy and this wicked rebellion,—slavery, which has scattered families, and desolated homes, and starved prisoners, and shot down men and women in cold blood,—slavery, which has eaten up the wealth of the country, and murdered your sons, or sent them to you as living skeletons,—slavery, this fiend, has now slain your president. Slavery is the assassin. It is the same spirit that has ruled the rebellion from the beginning. It began with the hanging of John Brown, and it has gone on demanding ever fresh and greater horrors to feed upon, until it ends with the murder of Abraham Lincoln. The awful laws of dramatic unity, stricter in the actual than in any fictitious tragedy, could not spare it this result, even though itself may have begun to shrink from the horror of it. It could not be permitted that this war, originated and fed by such a spirit, could end, and leave even a tradition of chivalry or honor or heroism on the side of slavery. All Southern valor and skill and self-sacrifice and devotion, which might otherwise have challenged and won the admiration of the world and posterity, are now swept from human memory by the infamy of this transcendent crime. Henceforth, through all history, the rebellion is branded as assassin. And slavery, which instigated and sustained the rebellion, has, by the law of its own necessities, brought it helplessly bound to this infamous end; and so it is forever proclaimed before all the world how purely evil and inhuman and diabolical a thing slavery is. It is the divine law by which evil works its own destruction, and, in attempting to undermine the good, digs its own grave. "Their sword shall enter into their own heart."

B

And is not this, my friends, a hint of the *moral* of this tragedy? Whether we needed the lesson or not, is it not clear to us now, that we cannot safely leave in the soil, anywhere in all the land, the smallest seed or root or filament or atom of that wrong against God and man out of which all this crime and curse of treason and war and assassination have grown? This may have been the last, desperate struggle of the monstrous wrong in its mortal agony, but it shows us that, until dead and utterly exterminated, it carries with it satanic stealth and violence and murder. And secondly, is it not plainly taught us that, if we cannot trust the spirit of this evil so long as the evil is anywhere above the ground, so we cannot safely trust, in any efforts at reconstructing the Republic, the men who have been conspirators for the defence and extension of this evil,—that we cannot trust them in any offices of the nation or the states? They must be outlawed. They challenged and defied the federal government, they threw down the gauntlet against justice and for slavery: they have failed, and now let them abide the issue. Let justice be done: pardon and freedom and suffrage for the mass of the people, for white and for black; the penalty of treason or the outlaw's fate for the leaders. Not alone justice, but gratitude and honor and a true magnanimity and mercy demand, that, in our reconstructed Union, we shall not hold off at arm's length those who have been our firmest and most faithful friends in the South, and refuse to them the equal rights of the government which they have helped to maintain, while we take to our compassionate bosoms the men who, so long as they were able, stood against us as our enemies, and who

even now may stab us as we lean confidingly upon them.
There is room for honorable magnanimity and for christian
mercy, without risking the very cause for which our armies
have fought and our victories been gained. We want no
unholy passion, no vindictive wrath; let the majesty of law
be maintained; let there be no belittling of the great
occasion by any assumption of the powers of retribution by
private hands; but there are eternal laws of divine justice
to be nationally vindicated for white and for black; and
when we talk of magnanimity, we must not forget the race
that has been waiting in patient suffering these many years
for the magnanimity of this nation, and by whose help we
have been lifted to a position where we have now the power
to be magnanimous.

Is it possible, my friends, that we needed this awful
calamity to teach us this lesson? to urge us to some duty
that we were shrinking from? to push us to the full completion of this dire work of war by the establishment of
absolute and impartial justice? Is it possible—is it not
possible—that even now we could not build a true and
lasting Union without this sacrifice, the greatest and highest
that we could make? that, even with these gates of victory
open, we could not enter the temple of perfect peace, unless
the blood of our president should sprinkle the threshold
and consecrate the altar? Let each ask and answer for
himself; and answering, heed the promptings of solemn duty.
Christianity was only a partial reform of Judaism until its
leader was put to death by the hands of wicked men on
Mount Calvary. Then it was transfigured, and became a new
religion. Jesus lived a holy and wonderful life, but not till

he was led to the cross did the hour come in which he was
to be glorified. And this, O friends, may be the hour in
which this nation is to be glorified. It may be, and God
grant it, that half-measures of justice will now be swallowed
up in absolute and complete equity ; that partial reform will
give way to thorough regeneration; and that the nation
henceforth will be no more the same, but transfigured and
impelled by a new spirit. Through our great leader, we
are crucified. God grant that we may also be glorified, even
as he is glorified ! Of all the days in the year, the assassins
chose Good Friday to strike their fatal blow,—the day that
their brother assassins, eighteen hundred years ago, put to
death the Redeemer in Judea. Auspicious omen! The
tomb shall not hold him. The stone shall be rolled away
from this sepulchre also. And he shall appear among us
again in another form, pleading for truth and justice and
humanity, so that our hearts shall burn within us by the
way; and in closet and council he shall still come to us, and
speak "Peace" to our troubled souls. One duty also,
chiefest of all, will he enjoin: "Lovest thou me? Feed
my lambs; feed my sheep,—the weak and little ones, the
poor, neglected, oppressed, whose bonds I loosed."

Friends, this is Easter Sunday. Already it is time we
were at the door of the sepulchre to await his coming, to
listen for his higher bidding. Let the night of darkness
and distraction and fear vanish. Lift up your eyes; behold
the glories of the resurrection morning.

April 16, 1865.

II.

DISCOURSE ON THE DAY OF THE FUNERAL RITES.

MY FRIENDS, this is not the hour for long or elaborate speech. We have come together by a natural and spontaneous impulse, that we may join, even at this distant point, in the funeral solemnities of our late honored President. Our hearts are too bitterly shocked and grieved, our souls too full of sadness, for many words: a sadness, not only for the great loss that our nation, and the world even, have sustained, but a still deeper sadness because of the infamous crime and lasting shame to our country through which this sudden loss has come; for not in the ordinary course of nature and Providence does the nation suffer this bereavement, but through the agency of a deed of the most atrocious wickedness. Providence permitted it,—but only as it permits, only as it does not interfere with, the freedom of the human will, even though, swayed by satanic purposes, that will should lie in wait for innocent blood, or lay its murderous hand upon the Lord's anointed. Providence permitted it: and the infinite Providence will neutralize and transform it, as it does all evil, into final good and blessing,—we cannot doubt that: and yet divine Providence, for the very reason that it is infinitely good and holy, must shrink in utter aversion and horror from the sight of such a crime. The whole race of humanity is stained by it, and the very heavens are blackened, and weep for shame.

But I would not use this hour to utter even the just indignation and anguish of horror that fill us at the cause of this national calamity and grief. Justice to society, the honor and progress of humanity, may in such a case demand that there be no act of human pardon; but with God — *with God* — while He looks down with a keenness of paternal sorrow, that we can have no conception of, upon the crime,— with God, there is yet always some way of forgiveness for the criminal, — because, what is not always the case with man, there is with Him always some way, at some time, in some world, for bringing even the greatest criminal back, through the path of repentance, to newness and purity of life. With Him also, with God, is almighty power in some way to overrule all evil, even the blackest and most grievous, to draw from it its poisonous and agonizing sting, and to transmute it by degrees into the pure gold of truth and integrity and holiness. None but the Infinite One has this power: and so to Him we turn in this hour, seeking through this thought, on the wings of this faith, to mount up, up, above all this earthly darkness and woe and sin and despairing grief — up to the unshaken, eternal, unchangeable wisdom and might of the Infinite, — up to such point of spiritual elevation that we can see how, amidst all the conflicts, and perplexities, and complexities, and evils, and crimes, and sorrows of our finite lives, an overruling, universal Law, holding them all firmly in its grasp, works out unswervingly its wise designs; and how, over all special wills and deeds, with their warrings and weaknesses and aberrations, there is one general will and providence, aiming always at the utmost possible good, and never moved from its path, never thwarted for a moment, by what passes on this little planet, among our little race.

Yes, my friends, in this hour of all hours do we need faith in God, — in a God who is a present Providence and Ruler in the earth, and whose designs cannot be circumvented by any wandering will, or disobedience, or even heaven-defying crime, of man. In God is our trust, our refuge, and our hope, — in the eternity of His Laws, in the eternity of His Love. Over all the failures and sins and crimes of men, the great Law still works on, taking up and solving all these lower disturbances in its higher spiritual harmonies. Look up, O friends, even from out of this depth of national humiliation and grief, — look up into the heavens, above the earth, above its clouds and ills, and see ever "beauty for ashes." See how, in the pure vault above our heads, the eternal stars come out, and take our little earth into their company, — take it with all its disorders into the harmony of the celestial spheres, its very perturbations being provided for and cancelled in their grander revolutions. And so we may ever read in the wise beneficence of the great providential laws, even in the midst of our strifes and wars and deeds too black to name, the everlasting gospel of "Peace on earth, good will to man." All things are transformed for man's eternal welfare, and the evil doers themselves are compelled to nullify their own purposes; their crimes, however black, and though wholly the result of human will and human depravity, and never foreordained by God, are yet not outside of His eternal laws, and are not unprovided for in His benign plan of the universe. No sooner is crime committed than it touches some secret spring in these infinite, all-embracing laws, which the wicked men who plotted it had no thought of, and which sets in motion moral forces that are freighted with sure retribution for them and sure overthrow of the evil principle and passion out of which their wickedness came. Or where we cannot see the operation of this benignant law, we can at least bow in silent trust, as we do before the infinite Providence to-day, with hands upon our lips reverently hushing all questions, all doubts, satisfied that the grand centre around which all these finite spheres of life revolve is Infinite Love, which is therefore amply able to cancel all their errors, to redeem all infamies,—satisfied that whatever else may go down, the Heart of the universe cannot fail;—

> " And so, by faith correcting sight,
> We bow before His will, and trust
> Howe'er they seem, He doeth all things right."

To-day the nation buries its president. And such a president! than whom we have had none better, none more honored and beloved since our first. If Washington was the father of our country, Lincoln was its savior. And in many respects he came nearer to the heart of the people than did even Washington. A gentle, kind, lovable man, who, in all the bitterness of this civil war, with all its political and personal strifes, has never said a harsh thing of any of his enemies North or South, and who never did a cruel thing in all his life. His faith in human nature and in the good intentions of even his worst foes, and his tenderness in judging others' conduct and motives, were almost pathetic in their simplicity. Perhaps he had not severity and roughness enough for the stern work that the time demands. And yet, as we look back from his grave upon this trait of his character, so christian in its type of mercy, so constant always in all his words and deeds, so forever characterizing him in all history as our *good* president, we can hardly wish that he had been otherwise. His few public faults, which were relative only to the times in which he had to act, all lay on the side of great virtues, and at any other time would have been great virtues. An honest, conscientious, unselfish, philanthropic man was he; thoroughly incorruptible; devoted with single, uncompromising aim to the good of his country and the interests of humanity; and believing most earnestly in the God-given equal rights and privileges of all men. Not an enthusiast, but wise; reticent of his opinions and public purposes, yet familiar, and unwillingly turning his ear from any comer; exquisitely modest and unassuming,—always Abraham Lincoln still, though president,—*the man* always more than, and above, the president; never in all the events of these years claiming anything for himself, but giving the credit ever to others, and to events, and to the people, whose servant he always called himself, and to God, whose will, without any affectation of piety, he meant religiously to follow. Not a rapid man in coming to an opinion, but coming surely, he never had to take a step backward through having taken a misstep; he never went farther than he saw to be clearly right, but always just as far as he saw, and held to his position, until

c

new light should lead still farther forward, with a heroic
persistency;—a man seeking new light, constantly progres-
sive, and meaning to do his whole duty; a man of great
sagacity, and knowledge of men, intuitively quick in perceiv-
ing the means necessary for any proposed ends, keen in the
use of arguments, believing in the application of absolute
principles to politics, and possessing large common sense
for devising the practical policies necessary for making the
application;—therefore a true and eminently successful
statesman.

And this man, thus gifted, thus devoted, has led the
country through four years of unexampled civil war and
peril to the final glory of military triumph, and to the very
verge of assured peace; and, crowning honor of all, under
God he has been the instrument of delivering from bondage
a whole race among us that former administrations of the
government for long years had helped to oppress,—a race
who now gaze wistfully after him as their ascended savior,—
while the country advances through this door, which his
hands have opened and no man's now can shut, to a new
career and to a glorious destiny,—free, united henceforth in
institutions and spirit as well as in form, and the hospitable
home and helper of universal humanity.

Here, my friends, in these capacities and in these opportunities and deeds, are the elements of a rare greatness as
well as goodness; and history, I believe, will adjudge that
Abraham Lincoln was not only our good president, but also
one of our few great presidents. Here are elements of
deed and character, which, if we will put them together,
not essentially different from what they were in his life, will

give us the hero that we have been asking for all through these years of war. The true hero is seldom entirely recognized when present. But it is of such characters as this that a nation's history makes up its most precious jewels.

And this man, thus gifted, thus devoted, thus trusted in, and followed, and beloved, the nation buries to day: buries him — oh, bitter memory! — from the assassin's fatal hand. Henceforth our cause is consecrated by his martyrdom. Bury him? We bury only what was the least and outermost part of him. While the stricken people all through the land, in city and in country, join in these obsequies over his grave, he himself is more vital in the nation than ever before. Already his spilled blood is coursing with quicker pulses in the veins of the country; and treason, conspiracy, and despotism, tremble before this dead president more than they did before him living. He reigns to-day in hearts that never admitted him before. People that laughed at him in life drop heavy tears on his bier, and wherever there is a heart that had a single spark of loyalty left, it is kindled into a generous, active patriotism now. Lifted up from the earth, he draws all men unto him. Bury him? We enthrone him! He is henceforth our leader more than when he led us in the flesh, — our leader now in the spirit. They have crucified him; the country, humanity, Heaven, glorifies him.

Farewell, departed form! and sweetly rest from the turmoil of war beneath the friendly sods of thy prairie home. Hail, risen and glorified spirit! not lost to earth, though gained to Heaven.

April 19, 1865.

III

THE CAPACITY AND HISTORICAL POSITION OF PRESIDENT LINCOLN.

The memorial of virtue is immortal: because it is known with God and with men. When it is present, men take example at it; and when it is gone, they desire it: It weareth a crown, and triumpheth forever, having gotten the victory, striving for undefiled rewards. Wis. of Sol. iv. 1, 2.

Again we are summoned together to give utterance in some more deliberate manner to our sense of national loss, and to express our reverence for the national leader and the man whom we have lost. Six weeks have passed away since the bloody crime was committed that brought us the bereavement. Yet it needs not that anything of praise or affection that was then said, in the first moment of indignant grief, be now unsaid. Not even the words of eulogistic love and admiration that were pressed burning from a nation's outraged heart, will give Abraham Lincoln so high a place in history, as will the sober pen of the historian, a hundred years from to-day, writing with cool nerve the simple facts of his life. For myself, the farther I get away from the inhuman scene of his death, the farther I go back of all the accidents and concomitants, whether of his death or his life, to the real man that he was, the more do I wonder and admire. He has left words and deeds and a finished work of statesmanship and philanthropy, which, aside from all interest excited by his tragic fate, worthily secure to him, not only the present gratitude and homage of the nation, but historic immortality among the few great names that America has produced. Washington, Jefferson, Franklin, Lincoln,—will not these be the four names that, a hundred years hence, will shine with most lustre in the first century of our national history?

I would speak to-day no mere eulogy. There is no need to exaggerate or to conceal. In discussing such a character we can afford to utter the simple, naked facts. All rhetorical adornment seems but tinsel where there is such pure gold. I would keep strictly within the limits of truth and soberness, while I attempt, though with very inadequate success, to bring together some of the elements by which Abraham Lincoln's capacity, and place in history, must be measured. We shall find, also, that in this life and death, is matter for such history as Shakspeare wrote, which records not only outward events and measures outward greatness, but traces in national events and through individual lives the course and conflicts of absolute, vital principles; and shows how men, though they die, yet triumph in their death, because over their graves the cause they lived for is lifted up out of the arena of conflict and passion, to receive ever after the undivided homage and reverence of the world. Abraham Lincoln, the man, is one of the noblest gifts of our Republic to history; but Abraham Lincoln, the martyr, sanctifies republican freedom and makes our history forever sacred.

In measuring the character and historical value of this man, the first question to be asked is, What was his individuality? that is, had he original power in himself? were there in his own being such elements of strength that he impressed himself strongly upon other men and upon events? did he have personal greatness and weight? And this question is put first, because the answer to it is most obvious, and leads us to one of the main elements of Abraham Lincoln's character and national strength.

We have had few public men in America—scarcely one, I think—more purely original,—scarcely one who relied more, or with greater safety and success, upon native, inborn capacity, and upon the individual convictions and experience developed out of native capacity. Few men, in any age or nation of the world, placed in so high a position, have borne its responsibilities so naturally and so easily, or, in the midst of great events and dangers, have assumed responsibility so naturally and borne it so safely. In the great crises of the war, we have sometimes asked indeed for more show of power in the executive branch of the government; we have wanted to be consciously led by the will of a strong man, and to see the display of that will in the nation. Yet all the while that we have been praying for a leader, this man has been really leading us. I doubt if we have ever had a president—I do not except even Jackson or Washington—who was more truly the leader and ruler of the people than Abraham Lincoln. And the fact that he took this position so easily, and held it so quietly, that the people were not conscious of his hand holding and guiding them, is additional and consummate proof that he possessed the individual,

native power that makes one a natural leader. He led
without even knowing it himself. He disclaimed all idea of
leadership,—disclaimed it in perfect sincerity; said that
the president was the servant of the people and only followed
to do their bidding. But in the very effort and claim to be
their servant, he became their master. Refusing to put
himself at the head of any party or clique, listening respect-
fully and sincerely to all, but deciding for himself and taking
the responsibility in his own hands at last, he became in
reality the head of the nation.

And this position he held, because of the inherent strength
and force of his individual character. When the war first
burst upon the country, and Abraham Lincoln — a Western
lawyer, with little general culture and experience in statesmanship — almost by accident was at the helm of affairs,
selected with no reference to the great events that were
coming, men began to look at each other with doubt and
anxiety; and prominent persons of the party that had elected
him wished that they could have foreseen, so that they might
have chosen a stronger man. But Providence foresaw, and
was wiser than the politicians would have been, or were.
They did at Chicago better than they knew. They were
thinking only of a temporary availability during an elec-
tioneering campaign, and so chose Abraham Lincoln for the
presidential candidate; Providence, foreseeing a four years
struggle with the power of slavery, was thinking of availability in its highest sense, and so let them choose him. For
had they foreseen, where would they have found their
stronger man? William H. Seward was then the foremost
statesman of the party. Does any one now regret that he

was not the successful candidate? As events have proved, does any one believe that he has comprehended the struggle with a keener insight or with a broader grasp? He has held the first place in the cabinet and done good service there; some of us have sometimes thought that he had too much influence with the president for the president's good—that he was in reality president. But when the facts are all known, we shall find that the Western lawyer was never overmatched in his cabinet by the shrewd, cultivated, experienced, philosophic statesman of New York. Nor would Chase have made a stronger president for the crisis. His policy, in some respects, from the outset might have been bolder and more radical; personally, in the early stages of the war, it might have suited you and me better; but it would have inevitably put him at the head of a party rather than at the head of the loyal nation; and with all our admiration and reverence for him, we may well doubt whether he could have led the country through these four years of perils on the right hand and on the left so safely as it has been led under its actual leader. We have had, too, the benefit of his strength in the cabinet.

And other strong men, officially and unofficially, have stood as advisers of the president. Yet he has stood the real head of the nation, clear and clean above them all. No ruler was ever readier to listen to opinions from all quarters, — to admit all comers, and give every class of men and every party and every individual citizen a chance to be heard. But all these opinions went through the crucible of his own keen judgment, and came out into deed through his own will, if they ever came out at all. His cabinet officers sometimes complained that they were not even advisers, but only clerks, so independently did he frequently act of them. During Buchanan's administration, and for many years preceding, the policy of the government and all its great measures were decided by a vote of the cabinet, the president making himself strictly the executive of the will of the majority. Lincoln, from the outset, made the cabinet only an advisory body, seeking their advice or not according to his feeling of need, and in any event reserving to himself the right of decision. Sometimes he consulted a part without the knowledge of the rest; sometimes took important steps without the knowledge of any of them. But equally, whether acting by their advice or not, the responsibility was always his, and he was willing and sought to bear it, not for ambition's but for conscience' sake, before the country and the world. Congress passed a resolution of censure against a member of his cabinet: immediately he sent a message to Congress, announcing that the acts censured were his,—and the country, though it had been clamorous against the secretary, said directly that the president was right. Again, a furious party were crying down the secretary of war for withholding supplies from, and secretly plotting against the success of, their favorite general: the president, in a public speech, said that he himself had done the deeds complained of,—and the people were silenced. He declared the report of a cabinet-officer to Congress to be his own, and changed it, if it ran counter to his own ideas. And so, generally, he never shrank from taking upon himself any responsibility in the conduct of affairs that the emergency demanded. He initiated measures and assumed powers that in any other

D

time but that of war would have been in clear contravention
of the Constitution; and sometimes his habit of free and
solitary action, even when there seemed to be no great
emergency, alarmed the friends of the administration and
excited the constitutional jealousy of Congress. And in
any other man almost, in a selfish and ambitious man, such
a habit would have been dangerous. But in him it was so
balanced by transparent integrity, and unselfish, conscientious
devotion to the country's good, that the people instinctively
felt, whatever the opposing politicians might say, that the
alarm was groundless and even ludicrous. Yet it was well,
perhaps, that there were such sharp critics even among the
friends of the administration, as Wade and Chandler and
Winter Davis, to keep the old moorings of the Constitution
and the powers and dignities of Congress in sight, that the
people might easily lay hold of them again, in the event of
a really dangerous man assuming arbitrary power.

Now these acts and ways of the late president are the
acts and ways of a man of large original individuality and
strength. Not speaking of them now either to censure or
to praise, but simply as evidence of character and capacity,
they denote a man of great personal power; of large native
resources; of inherent ability to lead and command,—a man
of independent thought and energy and will,—a man, who,
though standing among strong men, impressed them more
than he was impressed by them, and so showed himself
stronger than they all. He impressed himself also upon
events; and, though wisely accepting their teachings—indeed,
by accepting their teachings—kept himself always above
them, and held them in a manner within his control. He

was strong enough to disregard custom and precedent and fashion, the politic ways of more experienced statesmen, and the secret arts of diplomacy, and to walk in a path of his own appointing, — to hew out his way, indeed, as he went along. And this he did with no bluster of innovation, with no appearance of meeting antagonistic forces, but with the quiet modesty and easy self-possession and assurance of true greatness. He did it from the sheer greatness of his manhood, — from the sheer strength and power of the native stuff out of which the individuality of his manhood was developed. We have not always, I know, accorded to him this commanding ability. But history, I believe, will correct our decision : we are already correcting it ourselves.

Next, we are to inquire more particularly what were the elements of this large, commanding individuality ? through what special faculties came this general efficiency ?

First, as to the intellectual. Dividing the intellect into the intuitive, or philosophical, intellect; the imaginative, or poetical, intellect; and the logical, or practical, intellect, — we should not claim for Mr. Lincoln any remarkable develop-ment of the two former divisions. In the imaginative and poetical faculties, he was deficient. He seems to have had little appreciation of the beautiful in any of its forms. He was as plain and rugged in his style of writing and thought as in his person and manners. He was entirely wanting in intellectual enthusiasm. His state papers, for the most part, though on subjects dear to his heart and of great popular interest, have been cold and practical only, and though satisfactory in substance, have awakened little popu-lar emotion. More imagination would have enhanced his power. It would have given him an enthusiasm, a warmth, a consciousness something like the heroic of the magnitude of events and of his own part in them, which the people have missed, and to which they would have responded with a more buoyant patriotism. It might have made him even to their consciousness the leader and hero that he actually was, so that he could have carried the country with greater ease than he did through some of the valleys of despondency and over the mountainous difficulties of the four years' struggle.

Nor should we claim for President Lincoln any remarkable development of the intuitive, or philosophical, intellect. He was no metaphysician. He seldom traced even the great principles upon which he acted back to their absolute sources or grasped them in their theoretical relations. In establishing his principles, he did not go back farther than was necessary for the practical purpose in hand. He relied more upon observation and experience than upon intuition. Compared with Mr. Seward in respect to this. division of the intellect, he was inferior: yet perhaps the inferiority did not make him the worse leader for the times. Compared with Jefferson in this particular, he would fall far short; with Washington, he might stand on about the same level.

But his practical and logical intellect was extraordinary. He had wonderful greatness and quickness of understanding,—an immense amount of common sense. In this was concentrated the whole force of his mental nature : and here lay one of the main elements of his individual power. Seward stood far below him in this regard; and so, when it

came to affairs of practical statesmanship, the Western
lawyer distanced his philosophical competitor on the first
trial, though the latter had thirty years of public training
behind him. In amount of practical intellect, neither Jefferson, nor Washington, nor even Franklin, was his superior.
I think we have had no public man in America who, on this
point, surpassed him. It was this that made him the keen
and powerful logician, and the worthy antagonist, even in
their own field, of greater philosophers and more experienced
statesmen. It was this that gave him a style of oratory
more convincing than any grace of manner or beauty of
diction could have done : he had something sensible to say
and he made his auditor see it to be sensible ; no rhetorical
art could put things in writing more strongly than his plain
common sense did. It was this — this extraordinary amount
of practical common sense — that gave him his knowledge
of men, and his quick insight into motives and character,
and his ready understanding of the ways of managing men
and quietly moving great affairs. It was this that, in his
high position and among men of broad culture, more than
made up for any deficiency in the knowledge of books and
the polish of colleges. It was this in a great measure,
combined with his remarkable humor — which also belonged
to the practical side of his intellect — that kept the people
on such terms of cordial understanding with him, and held
them to him in such close bonds of sympathy and trust.
Whenever there was dissatisfaction or partial alienation, a
speech or a letter came, filled with such homely, honest
words of common sense, that they drew men to him in
admiration of his sagacity, and silenced, if they did not

convince. His letters to the Springfield Convention, and to Governor Magoffin and Mr. A. G. Hodges of Kentucky, are specimens of argumentative political epistles hardly to be matched elsewhere. They are decisive, and make answers impossible. So also was the characteristic argument with which he pricked the bubble of Douglas's oft repeated pro-slavery sophistry of popular sovereignty. "My distinguished friend," said he, "says it is an insult to the emigrants of Kansas and Nebraska to suppose that they are not able to govern themselves. We must not slur over an argument of this kind because it happens to tickle the ear. It must be met and answered. I admit that the emigrant to Kansas and Nebraska is competent to govern himself, *but I deny his right to govern any other person without that person's consent."* His public letters and speeches are filled with similar sharp thrusts of logic; and he has left words of wisdom and wit that the world will never allow to die,— words that will give him a place in history among the first order of men honored for practical sagacity and power.

But when we turn to President Lincoln's moral nature, we find a still richer field for admiration and study. In moral qualities he stood almost without a peer among the world's great rulers and magistrates. No living statesman surpasses him in that element of personal greatness that accrues from moral strength. In this regard, he goes above Jefferson and Franklin; Washington is his only rival among our chief historic names; and in some particulars he is superior even to Washington. The equanimity of Washington was some-times disturbed by the malicious charges and inventions of his enemies; his rare dignity and reserve gave way, and he

stormed with indignant passion. Lincoln, though he may
have had less of official and personal dignity, yet had a more
equable temperament. Amidst all the partisan and personal
strifes of these years of civil commotion and war — the
slanders and indignities and evil machinations of his foes, the
vexatious criticism and distrust and falling off of friends —
his natural serenity and self-command seem never for a
moment to have forsaken him. I do not think he has left a
harsh or bitter word against his worst or most annoying
enemy; for there was no harshness or bitterness in his heart,
not in its most secret corner. He was capable of feeling
only pity, charity, and forgiveness. Unconsciously he wrote
the motto of his own life in the phrase of his last Inaugural,—
"Malice toward none, charity for all."

There was, too, a wonderful warmth and tenderness in
his moral nature. The people felt the pulsations of a great
brotherly heart beating within that gaunt, ill-compacted
frame, and making even it almost beautiful. His eyes were
great deeps of sympathy and honest affection; transparent,
yet no one ever saw to the bottom of them. His mouth
moved naturally to expressions of sincerity and good-will;
and his whole face, which, when in repose, was heavy and
melancholic in its cast, was transfigured with a strange and
tender beauty, when anything touched the subtle wires that
made connection with his heart, and sent upward its thrilling
pulses: and his heart was always the first part of him to be
touched. Pressed on all sides by the gravest public cares
and anxieties, he could yet find time to write with his own
hand to a poor woman in Boston, who had given five sons
to glorious deaths for the republic on the field of battle, and

whose sixth was lying severely wounded, — a letter which, to that lone woman, will always be a more precious legacy of wealth than all the riches which a grateful government or a generous public could give her. After a wearying day in his office, burdened with dispatches to be read, with papers to be examined and judged, with personal calls and questions innumerable, private and public, to be disposed of, seeking finally, long past the accustomed hour, to retreat to his private room for rest, he hears without the door a sound like the hushed cry of a child. Immediately weariness is forgotten, the usher is summoned and asked, if a woman with a child in her arms is in the ante-room. "Yes, sir, — been trying three days to see you, and on a very important matter, if I may be permitted to say it," was the answer. "Let her come in at once," responded the president. And soon the poor woman goes out again, with light steps now, her hunger and weariness forgotten, and covering her baby with kisses and tears of joy; for she has saved her soldier son's life. Thus did our dear president never weary of kind and merciful deeds. He could not help doing them.

And this moral tenderness compensated in considerable measure for his want of intellectual enthusiasm, and sent some throbs of warmth even through his mental dryness and coldness. It shows itself in his official papers, otherwise so wanting in fervor, and gives to them sometimes a pleading, persuasive earnestness and pathos, that might almost draw the tears from an enemy. When his pen goes down to this part of his nature, his words, always clear and strong, come forth mellowed with beauty, and rise sometimes into real grandeur. What could be more gentle, or

more touching in its simple eloquence, than the closing
words of his first Inaugural address: "I am loath to close.
We are not enemies, but friends. We must not be enemies.
Though passion may have strained, it must not break our
bonds of affection. The mystic cords of memory, stretched
from every battle-field and patriot grave to every living
heart and hearthstone all over this broad land, will yet
swell the chorus of the Union, when again touched, as surely
they will be, by the better angels of our nature."

This natural kindness of his heart showed itself every-
where, in all his domestic and social and public life; made
him the good husband and father, as well as good president;
and held those who were his intimate friends very close to
him with a rare greatness of love. Combined with his sense
of justice and his democratic principles, it rose also to the
height of philanthropy, and made him, in the providence
of God, the natural and inevitable leader of this nation in
its struggle with the powers of despotism and slavery, and
the trusted and now glorified redeemer of an oppressed
and outraged race.

But not alone by these rare qualities was his moral nature
characterized. All the moral sentiments and faculties appear
to have been fully and symmetrically developed in him.
No vices are recorded against him; and this, in itself, indi-
cates a rare virtue. We should not credit him, perhaps, with
the most delicate moral sensitiveness. His moral strength
lay rather in principles and habits than in nicety of feeling.
He had a large and powerful conscience, which ruled his
own conduct with a puritanic severity; but he had no
moral squeamishness, which repelled him from all contact

F.

with vice itself and from vicious men. He knew very well
that the world, in the present ethical state of mankind,
could not be governed by saints alone,—that the good could
not withdraw from the bad, but must stand together with
them, in order that the whole may be made better as fast as
possible. He did not remove men from office, or decline to
appoint men to office, because of any bad habits they may
have had, provided their bad habits would not detract from
their usefulness for the work assigned them. It is reported—
and probably with truth—that, when, during the siege of
Vicksburg, some delegation asked for the removal of General Grant because of his alleged intemperate use of whiskey,
the President replied, that he would like to ascertain what
kind of whiskey General Grant was in the habit of using,
that he might give it to some of the other generals. Yet
the president himself was temperate to the degree of total
abstinence; and he made this reply, not because he was
insensible to the evil of intemperance in the army, but
because he believed, what has proved to be the case, that
General Grant, with the immense responsibility that was
placed upon him, would have strength to resist temptation,
and so give unimpaired his consummate ability to the salva-
tion of the republic. President Lincoln was no moral
Pharisee. He was a Pharisee in no respect. He had none
of the "I-am-holier-than-thou" spirit. He grasped the hand
of every man as a brother. He was no moral exquisite,
standing aloof from his kind, with nerves too delicate for
contact with men of common frailties.

Yet, though his moral nature was not of the extremely
sensitive order, it was extraordinarily strong and sure, and

was never harmed by contact with vice. He was eminently above being influenced by evil example. He had an integrity upon which the foulest slander of partisan strife has left no stain; an honesty that at once summoned and held the confidence of the country; a frankness and sincerity that astonished politicians accustomed to concealed and sinister ways; a simplicity of habit that excited the derision of fashionable and conventional circles of society; a conscientiousness that knew no indirection, and startled the habitués of political circles in Washington; an ambition that aimed only at his country's welfare, and saw only his country's glory; an unselfish, unswerving, unflagging devotion of himself and all his means and abilities to what he saw to be right; a humility that never knew pretence, and never even allowed him credit for his good deeds; and a moral courage that, though not bold at radical innovation, was never prevented from innovation by any thought of popularity or unpopularity, and which held to every step that had been taken from a conviction of its justice, and to every principle that had been adopted because it was right, with a firmness that was anchored to the very throne of God. Here are moral qualities that made Abraham Lincoln preeminently the moral leader for the times. When we sum them up, we have a greatness of moral nature for which we shall not soon find the peer among the great magistrates of the world.

President Lincoln's moral qualities rose naturally into the religious; and of the religious character of the man, we come, finally, to speak. But here he has a right to the reserve which covers every person's deepest and inmost life. Because we have put a man into a public position and made him our servant, it does not give us a claim to enter with him into his closet, to lurk as eaves-droppers for his prayers, or to sit in judgment on his religious emotions. I shall not seek to spy behind the sacredness of this private veil. It is the religious character of the man only so far as publicly manifest that we have any right or proper interest to examine.

And keeping within these limits, we should not say that President Lincoln had the finest spiritual quality. He was not a Fenelon, a Thomas a Kempis, a Channing, or an Edwards. He lacked the intuitional faculty, I judge, in spiritual things as he did in intellectual; and, as was necessary from his cast of mind, he approached religion from the ethical and practical side. With its metaphysics or its prophecies, its theologies or its ecstacies, its Transcendental visions or its Methodistic raptures, he did not trouble himself. His religion was on the broad level of common sense. His sharp logic and keen humor could not fail to perceive and prick some of the long-standing theological absurdities,—as when, in his reply to an ecclesiastical delegation who, in the common phrase of their faith, had expressed the hope that the Lord would be on his side, he said: "I have not given myself any care whether the Lord is on our side; but I do feel anxious that myself and the people should be on the Lord's side."

Whatever were his ecclesiastical associations or training, we may be sure that such a mind was thoroughly unsectarian and liberal. There was no cant in his religion; no meaningless professions of piety. He, clearly, believed more in performing duty than in subscribing to theologies,—believed in a religion of righteousness—of obedience to God and helpfulness towards man. I do not credit the account, recently published, of an interview had with him by some Western clergyman, in which phrases are put into the president's mouth that sound very much like the exclamations heard in an excited meeting of revivalists. They do not tally with his marked characteristics of calmness and religious sobriety; he was no spiritual, more than intellectual, enthusiast; and this account doubtless received its flavor of pious zeal from the fervid evangelical conduits through which it passed. Nor, on the other hand, do I give much weight to what I heard on better authority, in Washington,—that President Lincoln was a warm admirer of Theodore Parker, and in sympathy with that great heresiarch's rationalistic views of religion,—though, from the cast of Mr. Lincoln's mind, I should credit this report sooner than the other: I can well conceive that he would find much to attract him in Mr. Parker's plain, practical sense in religious things, and in the rugged, homely way in which he dealt with some of the metaphysical absurdities of theology. There was really much in common between the characters of the two men,—so much, that of this we may be sure: whatever Mr. Lincoln's theological views were, and though it is not very probable they were in agreement with Mr. Parker's—quite likely he had not even read Mr. Parker's books—yet he would not have been frightened away, by any theological heresies of Mr. Parker, from admiring the sturdy moral courage of the man, or sympathizing with his efforts for the advancement of public morals and the elevation of humanity. Outwardly, President Lincoln was connected with the Presbyterians,—

that is, when he had leisure from public duties, he went to a Presbyterian church, and probably, without giving much thought to the matter, accepted in the main the doctrines there preached; but he was not a member of any church, and not an habitual attendant on the services of any. He was too broad to be a zealot of any sect; too practical to care much for the creed of any. He believed in a religion of work and duty.

Yet he was also a man of prayer, and faith, and trust. This country has hardly had a president who tried more sincerely to know and to do God's will; or who had a stronger belief in an overwatching and overruling Providence. When he said in respect to the progress and issues of the war, that God alone could claim to have controlled events, we see that the language in his mouth was no common-place of piety, and no mere convenient phraseology, easily used, as an apology for some unexpected or uncomprehended turn of affairs; but that the words expressed what he really meant and believed. More and more he came to consider himself as but an instrument in the hands of the Almighty.

His faith, it is true, was of conviction, rather than of temperament; his trust, the lesson learned through the stern tasks of an eventful life, rather than the childlike instinct of dependence. He had no ecstacies of faith. It was not given him to see spiritual visions. His religion did not fly; it had to walk the whole dusty way of life; it kept him close to the duty of earth, seldom allowing him even a glimpse of the height or splendor of heaven. We could wish, for his own joy, that his trust had been more intuitional;

that his spiritual temperament had been more ardent and hopeful; that the severe tasks of duty had been sometimes relieved by the prophetic imagination of coming glory. Yet, though not, by nature, of a peculiarly religious organization, he did come to a very sublime height of religious faith,—came to it through years of patient toil and endurance and suffering and brave fidelity to duty. We have had presidents who were more punctual in religious observances; but we never had one who believed more really in God, or more truly walked with Him in daily life. In the speeches and official papers of no former president, has religious faith shown itself to be so vital an element of character and of official conduct. From the day that he took leave of his neighbors in Illinois and requested them to remember him in their prayers, to the morning that his soul, through ruffian violence, was released from its weary, toil-worn body, his life was inspired, and sustained, and borne up higher every day, by this firm trust in God. Literally, he believed himself to be president of the republic "under God." His utterances of faith are sometimes of the Cromwellian order. Still, there was no rapture of divine communion, no enthusiasm, no fanaticism. There was stern self-denial and self-consecration; but no joyous abandonment of self to religious emotion. He made vows before God, and was in agony of travail until they should be accomplished. His will was utterly surrendered to the divine will; but it was the conscious self-surrender of a strong man to Almighty power and wisdom, rather than the instinctive nestling of a dependent child in the arms of Infinite love.

But, though with never ceasing strain upon his will, and

with a sense of duty never relaxed, he had to climb the whole rugged ascent to his height of faith, what a sublime height it was when once attained! His last inaugural address measures a majesty and comprehensiveness of religious faith of which we shall hardly find the like among all the great civil magistrates of the world, living or dead. It reminds us of Cromwell's official speech; but it surpasses the papers of England's Great Protector, since it rises above all taint of bigotry and all color and warmth of partisanship. Unique as a State paper, we shall with difficulty find for it a fitting comparison save in the utterances of Moses, Isaiah, and Paul. Here is a faith which has come "out of great tribulation," and washed its robes, and made them white in the blood of sacrifice; a faith which "through much tribulation" has climbed very close to the portal of the kingdom of God. Let the stealthy assassin strike when he will. Any moment will be too soon for the nation; but for such a faith, earth can never too soon pass away: for Heaven is already won.

The memorial of this man, my friends, is with us. Great in personal influence and power, great in logical and practical ability, great in all moral and humane faculties, great in religious faith, Abraham Lincoln takes his position by unquestionable right in the calendar of exceptional great men. The leader of one of the four greatest civil powers of the world in a triumphant contest against the most gigantic rebellion that the world has known; the representative of democratic liberty in a fierce struggle for national existence with aristocracy and despotism; the emancipator of millions of slaves, and, through the connection of events, the practical destroyer of the institution of slavery throughout the whole territory of the United States; the martyr, slain in the hour of his triumph by the consummate wickedness of the cause he had contended against, and sealing his testimony to democratic liberty with his blood,—he will take his place in history, not only among the men of rare greatness, but among the great men who had also rare opportunities, and filled them with rare achievements. Great in endeavor and in power, great always in goodness, he was equally great in fortune and success. To his name the muse of history will affix the title,—the Preserver of the American Union; the Destroyer of American slavery; the Representative Man of American Democracy. The memorial of his virtue is immortal: being "known with God and with men." Present, it was our example and guide; gone, we desire it: "it weareth a crown and triumpheth forever, having gotten the victory, striving for undefiled rewards."

National Fast, June 1, 1865.

IV.

THE DRAMATIC ELEMENT IN THE CAREER OF ABRAHAM LINCOLN.

For where a testament is, there must also of necessity be the death of the testator: for a testament is of force after men are dead. Hebrews ix. 16, 17.

I owe, perhaps, an apology for venturing to renew a theme on which so much has already been spoken, and for attempting to say to-day what might have been more appropriately said last Thursday, had not the subject grown under my pen into unforeseen proportions. But it is sweet to linger in the fragrance of a good man's memory. The part, moreover, that Abraham Lincoln has acted in our history can never become old or worn. It is a career upon which historians will ever love to dwell, and which will never lose its charm for the people. And after all that has been spoken and written concerning him, there is yet one phase of his wonderful life and tragic destiny which has great attractiveness, and which I have hinted at once or twice in previous discourses, but which, so far as I have seen, has not anywhere been fully developed or much noticed. Mr. Sumner, in his eulogy just spoken, touches more closely upon what I refer to than any other writer or speaker whose words have come

to my eye; but the object he had proposed to himself did
not allow him to more than skirt the border of this phase
of the great theme.

The point of view that I have in mind, is *the perfect dramatic unity and progress of Abraham Lincoln's life;*—the
wonderful line of destiny, or of providence, by which his
career, from his birth to his death, was unfolded, in all its
parts and acts, and through all its shiftings of place and
scene and time, on the thread of a single vital truth, and to
a single moral end. This life moves across the stage of
history with the dramatic march of one of Homer's heroes.
The stern demands of ancient Grecian tragedy were not
more observed by its great artists in their greatest works,
than they have been observed in the actual life of this
American president. Here must be no side issues; no con-
founding of moral lessons; no division and distraction of
one prevailing moral purpose and force; no departure, amid
whatever private or professional or domestic episodes, or
whatever change and variety of action, from the one truth
which this individual career from its outset was chosen to
embody and to teach for humanity: from its entrance on the
stage of earthly being to its exit, this life must be moved
by one inexorable purpose and will, and march to one inevitable fate,—in order to print upon the heart of the world one
of the grandest truths of human civilization and government
and progress.

This is our theme. But why bring it here, and make it a
subject of religious meditation? It may belong to the
dramatist and the poet, it may serve the uses of the lecture-
room and the magazine, but why bring it to the church?

Because, first, there is a providence behind the scenes—the hidden, infinite manager of the great drama. The ancients called it fate, destiny; we call it Providence, God, the Infinite Spirit. Abraham Lincoln, though self-possessed to an extraordinary degree, though having great independence and originality of being, and native resources and capacities very largely at his command, was yet impelled, as few men have been, by a power beyond his own,—possessed, used, chosen for a special work, by a spirit above himself. And, secondly, I bring the theme here, because of the grand moral importance to humanity of the truth which his life was selected thus dramatically to unfold and teach.

And what is this truth? It is the truth of republican freedom, simplicity, and equality; in one word, the truth of Democracy, as theoretically stated by Jefferson in the opening sentences of the Declaration of Independence. By the strict line of this truth, the life of Abraham Lincoln, act by act, and scene by scene, was developed, from the day his eyes first saw the light in a log-cabin on the western frontier of civilization, to the day when, as president of the United States, standing at the very topmost height of official position and honor, he was slain by the hand of an assassin, and those eyes closed forever to mortal things. To this truth he was born; to it he was apprenticed by the necessary conditions of his lot, during all the years of his boyhood and youth; at manhood it became his property purchased by conviction; it stamped henceforward his whole character, and all his personal, social, and professional habits; when he was called into political life, this was at once his creed and the central principle of all his measures and acts; and

when this truth was challenged and defied by rebellion to
the government founded upon it, then he, seemingly by
accident, yet inevitably, became the leader of the loyal hosts
in the fierce struggle with despotism and slavery,—led
them to triumph, and, in the hour of triumph, fell: fell that
he might have the greater triumph,—as the Greek tragedians
made their heroes fall, in order that they might ascend to
Olympus and to the society of the gods;—fell that he might
seal his testament to this truth of republican freedom, simplicity, and equality, with his blood, and sanctify it henceforth
as the solemnly established polity of the nation. Is not
here a life-drama such as is seldom enacted on this earth?

But let us bring out some of its features in fuller relief.
Let us see how, in every part of its course, this career is
vitalized, and its direction and progress determined, by the
truth I have stated,— see how close the hidden, inimitable
Artist ever holds it to the one purposed aim,—how statelily
and solemnly it advances, by steps that seem almost to know
whither they tend, to the inevitable tragic end.

The drama opens in the rudest and humblest condition of
democratic life,— the farthest possible removed from wealth
and culture, and from any influences that may have been
transmitted across the seas from the forms and refinements
of monarchical civilization. Not amid the schools and cities
and growing luxuries of the East, but in the far West, where
nothing is yet established but the pure democratic idea,
must the hero be born who is to testify for that idea through
life and by death. He must be born of nothing but pure
democracy. The world must see that this future republican
ruler owed nothing by birth save to republican freedom,

simplicity, and equality. Therefore he is born in a hut without floor, with but one room, with no articles of luxury, with very few even of comfort or necessity; born to toil and poverty; born of parents having no lineage, no learning, no library,—having nothing but a little spot of soil, and a rough shelter over their heads, and honest hearts, and hard working hands. Yet according to the theory of the country written in the Declaration of Independence, and partially established by the revolution, those parents are a part of the sovereignty of the land; and from their loins must be born the strong man who is to be leader and ruler of the nation through the severest contest that Democracy has ever known, and who is to testify to all history, and throughout all time, for the truth of the democratic idea.

But the contest against Democracy has already begun. There is an institution in the land that flagrantly denies its most fundamental principles,—an institution of caste, inequality, oppression, and despotism. This institution has spread out to the frontier settlements. It is closing around that democratic hut, menacing its prosperity, its virtue, and the precious promise it holds. Slavery joins issue with the democratic idea in Kentucky, and threatens utterly to overwhelm it. But the times are not yet ripe for the great struggle; the hero is still a boy; the strength and integrity that his honest parentage and home have given him must be saved from contamination. The drama is just beginning. Not prematurely must the crisis be developed. The parents, indeed, do not thus reason with conscious reference to the future: but the genius of the republic is jealously guarding its hero; the prophetic Spirit of Truth, sitting calm behind the scenes, will not permit the whole future to be changed and robbed at this dangerous point. The little spot of land, which slavery was already beginning to envelop and impoverish, is sold; the rude home is abandoned; the parents escape from the snares and dangers of slaveholding Kentucky, and seek across the Ohio, still farther in the wilderness, a new home, but on free soil.

And now still further is our hero trained for the stern tasks of democratic sovereignty before him. It seems as if he must understand every atom of that sovereignty, by going through the condition of every individual constituent of it, before he can be ready to assume it in his own person for the great ends designed. Hence he must exhaust every democratic occupation from the most menial to the most honored. He is a pioneer, and day after day, with sturdy blows, cuts a way through the forest to his home and to the land that is to feed him; he is a farmer, and by the sweat of his brow gathers his daily bread from the soil; he is a mechanic, and helps build the family house and its furniture; he is a famous rail-splitter, and fences the farm with his own hands; he is a flatboatman down the Mississippi; he is a clerk in a store; he is a militia captain, and has a little touch of war in the Indian troubles of the frontier; he sets up in business by himself as a country trader; he is postmaster, land-surveyor, and finally lawyer and legislator.

And all this time, too, he is gathering knowledge,—not in schools and colleges and lyceums and public libraries, but out among the Western forests and prairies; gleaning from nature, from life, and from the few books to be found among his scattered neighbors or bought with hard-earned savings;

laboring over his books in solitude by his democratic fireside, with his solitary democratic brain; — gathering knowledge, not to veneer over weakness and poverty of capacity, not enough even to cover and conceal the rugged fibre and homely solidity of the native stuff from which his being is made; all his knowledge is perfectly assimilated and used by his nature: for this man, born out of the loins of pure Democracy, and destined to be the leader of American Democracy in a deadly contest for national existence and to die its martyr, must be purely American and democratic through every nerve and fibre and pulse of his being.

But again the scene changes. The great struggle between Democracy and Despotism is approaching. The hosts are preparing on either side for the combat, and the destined leader of freedom must come forth into the public arena. Already in Congress he had voted steadily for freedom and equality in the national territories, and even at that early day had tried to make the national capital free soil. But now the contest had thickened, and the smell of blood was already in the land. The virgin soil of Kansas was the prize. Should it be polluted and ruined by the demon of slavery, or given in pure wedlock to freedom? The plot against Democracy begins to unfold its horrors: the "coming man" must now come. Unavoidably he is drawn from his retirement into the political field; and, although several years have yet to pass before he is hailed as leader, his powerful sword can never be sheathed again.

In the contest concerning Kansas, and in the famous Senatorial campaign with Stephen A. Douglas, which grew out of the Kansas conflict, it is remarkable how sharply the lines were drawn between freedom and slavery; how the debates constantly turned on this one point; and how radical and thorough Mr. Lincoln's utterances always were as the chosen champion of liberty. It is to be noticed, too, how he uniformly planted himself on the broad ground of the Declaration of Independence,—that is, of free and equal government for all classes and races; and he attacked slavery, because slavery attacked this invincibly true and fundamental principle of the Republic.

And at this point in the development of this dramatic history, we come to a very important and rarely noticed fact,—the key of the wonderful drama. Abraham Lincoln was the first politician or statesman who publicly proclaimed the doctrine of the "irrepressible conflict" of ideas between the South and the North. This he did on the 17th of June—the anniversary of the battle of Bunker Hill—1858, in a speech to the State Convention of Illinois, which nominated him for Senator against Douglas. That speech opened almost with the words now become so famous and familiar: "A house divided against itself cannot stand. I believe this government cannot endure permanently half slave and half free. I do not expect the Union to be dis-solved—I do not expect the house to fall, but I do expect it will cease to be divided. It will become all one thing or all the other." And this was the beginning of that noted Senatorial campaign, which was but preliminary to the Presidential campaign. It was the striking of the key-note of this great American contest; it was the clarion voice of the true, destined leader, summoning the hosts of freedom to his standard. For, mark you again, this was the first

G

political utterance of the doctrine of the irrepressible conflict between freedom and slavery, declaring that one of the
antagonists, even in the domain of the States, must yield
before the other. The moral reformers—the abolitionists—
had declared it ; but no statesman or leading politician
proclaimed it before Abraham Lincoln. It was he that first
took up and ingrafted upon the politics of the country the
moral ideas of the abolition reformers. He made this
remarkable speech several months before Mr. Seward took
the same idea, clothed it in philosophic shape, and christened
it by the name of " irrepressible conflict."

Can we longer wonder that Abraham Lincoln should be
the chosen leader of the hosts of democracy and freedom,
when this conflict comes to arms ? that he, the first statesman who announced the divine necessity of the moral conflict, should be summoned to represent divine justice in the
martial struggle, and to give thereto the costly testimony
of his life ? Not otherwise could the drama preserve its
unity. Blind fate, destiny, could have made no other choice.
Shall Providence be less wise than destiny ? Shall the prophetic, preparing, managing Spirit, be balked of its purpose ?
Shall a mighty national contest, involving national existence
and the virtue and happiness of millions of human beings,
be subject to accident ? its sublime end postponed or
thwarted by some political marplot ? No ! Providence is
as grandly steady as destiny or fate ; and not more inevitably, in the old Greek tragedy, did the fate-impelled hero,
at the proper moment, come upon the stage, than did Abraham Lincoln, in the dramatic ripeness of events, assume the
political leadership of this nation. Consciously or uncon-

sciously, when the clash of arms had come, the hosts of
loyalty and liberty could only rally around the man whose
voice had first uttered the true battle-cry. And therefore
it was that, when that moment came, we found Abraham
Lincoln, the leader that democratic freedom had been prepa-
paring in the West, in the President's chair at Washington,
and Commander-in-chief of the army and navy of the United
States.

And now events hasten more rapidly to the grand
dénoucment. Yet, like Hamlet, the hero hesitates. He
dreads the awful conflict. He shrinks, as it were, from the
very greatness of the task imposed upon him. Already,
too, villany lurks in his path, — assassination is dogging his
steps; and he walks henceforth as if burdened with a mys-
terious, foreboding consciousness of his destiny. In his
kindly, democratic nature, there should be, and is, no taste
for civil war and blood. He tries to conciliate, — puts forth
his arm to avert the rushing fates: he holds the chalice of
the Constitution to the white, maddened lips of the foe.
But all in vain. With boastful, furious words, the cup is
dashed to the ground: "We have a new Constitution,
founded on the divine right of slavery, — we fight for it, and
take and give no quarter!" And so freedom's leader is
held to his divinely purposed work, — defied by despotism,
until forced in self-defence into the impregnable citadel of
equal justice.

Yet the steps were all taken, not in passion, not in routed
haste, but deliberately and with dignity; some of us thought
too slowly and hesitatingly taken, and feared lest freedom
would be betrayed. But the great Dramatist knew better

than we,—knew the metal of the man; and knew he would not, could not, yield the principle to which his life had been, as it were by solemn vow, devoted.

Months before, in his contest with Douglas, with inspired earnestness, and in the old Roman spirit of absolute self-consecration to the highest welfare of the Republic, he had exclaimed:

"Think nothing of me; take no thought for the political fate of any man whatsoever, but come back to the truths that are in the Declaration of Independence. You may do anything with me you choose, if you will but heed these sacred principles. You may not only defeat me for the Senate, but you may take me and put me to death. * * * * I charge you to drop every paltry, insignificant thought for any man's success. It is nothing. I am nothing. Judge Douglas is nothing. But do not destroy that immortal emblem of humanity—the Declaration of Independence."

And again, on his way to Washington, in the old Independence Hall in Philadelphia, after inquiring what great sentiment it was in the Declaration there adopted which held the Colonies so firmly together in the revolutionary struggle, he answered, "It was that sentiment which gave liberty, not alone to the people of this country, but I hope, to the world, for all future time; it was that which gave promise that in due time the weight would be lifted from the shoulders of all men,"— and then he added,— "If this country cannot be saved without giving up that principle, I was about to say I would rather be assassinated on this spot than surrender it,"—and closed the remarkable speech with the solemn words: "I have said nothing but what I am willing to live by, and if it be the pleasure of Almighty God, die by." It was not in the nature of the man who had given himself to the whole truth of republican government with such vows as these, and whom the angel of the Republic was guarding for her highest service and greatest glory, to betray the sacred office for which he had thus received Heaven's commission. He was cautious; he saw every difficulty in the way; for a time it seemed as if he reasoned with destiny; but he could not betray the cause so solemnly committed to his hands.

He was mortal, indeed, and with all the care in preparing him for his high office, it was impossible that he should escape entirely all infection of the evil from which the whole nation suffered. He still had some respect for the local laws of slavery. And so the conflict must go on in him, as in the nation, until he should be purified by the fires of battle from all taint of the evil, and be lifted clear above all its entanglements, ready to strike the fatal blow with full moral strength. Observe, too, that consistently with his past record and training, he came to the contest, not as an abolitionist *per se*, but on the broad ground of democracy. He was an emancipationist because a true democrat. He believed in freedom and equality for all, and therefore for the black man. He came to the conflict not avowedly to destroy slavery, but to save democratic government; and he destroyed slavery because incompatible with the continued existence of democratic government. The one is the broader position, and necessarily includes the other. Democracy necessitates abolitionism. This is the truth he is to proclaim to the world, and lead on to victory.

And now see the solemn steps of the grand march. We

shall notice that there is no retrograde movement,—that there is really no delay,— that every step comes in its place with the sublime constancy of fate, but also with the paternal, humane promise of a tender Providence; and that every step lifts the nation upward upon higher and broader ground, and nearer to the glory of its final triumph. Even in the first Inaugural Address, though conciliatory and seeking in some respects by compromise to avert the conflict, the key-note of democratic faith and assurance is sounded. "Why," said the President, "should there not be a patient confidence in the ultimate justice of the people? Is there any better or equal hope in the world? In our present differences, is either party without faith of being in the right? If the Almighty Ruler of events, with his eternal truth and justice, be on your side of the North, or on yours of the South, that truth and that justice will surely prevail, by the judgment of this great tribunal of the American people." We passed these words by at the time with little notice; but now that the drama is complete, they sound like the solemn utterances of the chorus in ancient tragedy, pronouncing upon the gathering combatants the warning and the judgment of the gods. It was the presiding, oracular genius of the Republic that uttered them, giving judgment in advance.

Again, in the first message to Congress, dated July 4, 1861, though slavery is not directly attacked, there are brave sentences that strike at its root, and that must one day strike the fetters from all men's limbs. "This is essentially a people's contest. On the side of the Union it is a struggle for maintaining in the world that form and substance of government whose leading object is to elevate the condition of men; to lift artificial weights from all shoulders; to clear the paths of laudable pursuits for all; to afford all an unfettered start and a fair chance in the race of life." None but the Western pioneer, cradled in poverty, and, by his own sturdy hands and the "fair chance" that democratic institutions put into them, hewing his way into public position by a purely democratic path, could have uttered these words from the Presidential chair. Already we see in them the promise of a united and emancipated country. These are the same syllables that, by a little change of articulation, are to pronounce Richmond fallen, and the slave of South Carolina free.

In the message of December, 1861, there is an elaborate discussion, on principles of political economy, of the question of capital and labor,— in which the pure democratic ground is taken, that labor is superior to capital, and must be free and own capital, and not capital, labor. The discussion seemed to us abstract and ill-adapted to the pressing emergency of the hour; but we see now how fittingly it takes its place in the great struggle to complete the loyal argument. It is the bud of emancipation in the loyal border states. It is an appeal to prudent, thinking men, on grounds of industrial prosperity and self-interest. It brings the reenforcement of material and social well-being to the cause of divine justice. Hear, too, how at the close, the grand choral strain comes in again, giving utterance to the sublimer principles that underlie the irrepressible conflict, and summoning the contestants again to the bar of future judgment.

" This [the free system of labor] is the just, and generous, and prosperous system, which opens the way to all, gives hope to all, and consequent energy, and progress, and improvement of condition to all. No men living are more worthy to be trusted than those who toil up from poverty,— none less inclined to take or touch aught which they have not honestly earned. Let them beware of surrendering a political power which they already possess, and which, if surrendered, will surely be used to close the door of advancement against such as they, and to fix new disabilities and burdens upon them, till all of liberty shall be lost. * * The struggle of to-day is not altogether for to-day; it is for a vast future also."

Closely following—only three months later—a special message is sent to Congress, recommending the passage of a resolution by which the federal government shall be authorized to cooperate by pecuniary aid with any state that will enact gradual abolition of slavery. Two months afterward, in a public proclamation, attention is called to this resolution, which was adopted by Congress, and the states most interested are earnestly appealed to, to avail themselves quickly of its privilege. Says the President,—

"You cannot, if you would, be blind to the signs of the times. I beg of you a calm and enlarged consideration of them, ranging, if it may be, far above partisan and personal politics. This proposal makes common cause for a common object, casting no reproaches upon any. It acts not the Pharisee. The change it contemplates would come gently as the dews of heaven, not rending or wrecking anything. Will you not embrace it? So much good has not been done by one effort in all past time, as in the providence of God it is now your high privilege to do. May the vast future not have to lament that you have neglected it."

And so the chorus echoes back with added intensity the

divine plea of impartial justice that was the sublime burden
of the previous message.

In the regular message of December, 1862, the same subject is taken up again, and discussed more elaborately and
with greater scope. It is now proposed that Congress
shall not wait for the states to accept, at their option, its
offer of pecuniary aid toward emancipation, but shall initiate
emancipation. An amendment to the Constitution is recommended, by which slavery shall be gradually, yet entirely,
abolished in all the states and throughout the country. But
the great import of the paper was not so much what it
recommended — for its plan of emancipation was too heavily
conditioned to be practically available — as the fact that the
abolition of slavery was for the first time boldly and seri-
ously discussed, and made the most important topic, in a
regular Presidential message. More memorable still is the
message for its closing words, in which the chorus of the
drama again speaks, inspired by the genius of republican
freedom, who thus urges her champions up to the true battle
ground, and holds the now fast developing action close to
its divine intent. Hear the deep, stately, measured tones,
as they seem to come from the distant heavens :

"The dogmas of the quiet past are inadequate to the
stormy present. The occasion is piled high with difficulty,
and we must rise with the occasion. . * * We must disenthrall ourselves, and then we shall save our country. * *
No personal significance or insignificance can spare one or
another of us. The fiery trial through which we pass will
light us down in honor or dishonor to the latest generation.
* * * We — even we here — hold the power and bear
the responsibility. In giving freedom to the slave we assure-

freedom to the free — honorable alike in what we give and what we preserve. We shall nobly save or meanly lose the last, best hope of earth. Other means may succeed; this could not, cannot fail. The way is plain, peaceful, generous, just, — a way which, if followed, the world will forever applaud and God must forever bless."

But this paper coupled with its plan of gradual abolition the principles of compensation and voluntary colonization. Its proposed method of action was not so lofty as the spirit that inspired it. The noble goal aimed at condemned the halting effort. It was not for any such imperfect result that this mighty contest was proving the metal of the nation. The human instrument was not so far-sighted as the Providence which wrought through him, — the actor not so wise as the manager behind the scenes. Yet he is faithful and true, and submits himself with unwavering loyalty to the teaching of events and of God: and with ever lengthening and bolder paces he goes forward. One after another all imposed conditions of emancipation drop away. Compensation, gradualism, colonization, vanish and become obsolete ideas; and the champion stands, clean from all alloy of the evil he is to annihilate, alone with God and justice.

In August, 1861, he had modified General Fremont's proclamation of emancipation in Missouri to conciliate Kentucky. In May, 1862, he had countermanded General Hunter's decree of abolition in the department of the South, only because he reserved the great right for himself and would not allow it to be frittered away powerlessly, and with little moral effect, by subordinates. It is evident in the very order of countermand that he begins to see clearly what the line of duty and destiny must be. He appeals to the in-

surgent states, in the words already quoted, to smooth the
way to peaceful emancipation by voluntarily acceding to the
logic of events and to the plain intent of divine Providence.
Even as late as the 13th of September, he had received a
religious deputation from the city of Chicago, appointed to
urge him to declare emancipation by military proclamation,
and replied to their arguments with such a strong array of
objections to the measure that the deputation had departed
in great doubt as to his adopting it. But it is as clear as
noonday now, that the President had been debating the
measure in his own mind for months, and marshalling the
arguments for and against it, and that, in this interview, he
summed up the difficulties in the way, as they had presented
themselves to him, in order to draw forth, if possible, from
the deputation, new light upon the question. He also sig-
nificantly added at the close of the conference: "I can assure
you the subject is on my mind, by day and night, more than
any other. Whatever shall appear to be God's will I will
do." And now God's will is rapidly revealed to him,— not
through miraculous interposition, for, as he says, "these are
not the days of miracles"; but through an earnest desire to
"ascertain what is possible, and learn what appears to be
wise and right." Events are his instructors. The spirit of
Almighty Justice, unfolding its high purpose more and more
in the daily history of the struggle, is his teacher. He
consults his cabinet for suggestion, not for advice. Upon
him Heaven has put the responsibility, and he will decide
and bear the weight of the decision alone. And the decision being made, the duty clear, on the 22d of September, he
issues the preliminary declaration, and gives the final warn-

ing to the rebellious states; and on the 1st of January, 1863, appears the great Proclamation of immediate emancipation.

The critical blow has now been struck. The deed is done for which all before has been only preparation: and all that comes after — emancipation in the border states, the enlistment of negroes in the army, the Freedmen's Bureau, the anti-slavery amendment to the Constitution — is only the gathering up of the fruits of that victory and making it secure forever. The issuing of the Proclamation was the crisis in the drama; and so when that blow was given, the embattled hosts rushed to the conflict with a more furious and deadlier onset. It was now life or death to the foe and slavery, life or death to the nation and freedom. But through all the deathly contests on the martial field, and through all the struggles on the equally dangerous field of politics, threatened by foes and importuned by friends, the president never recedes from that decree. "The promise," he says, "being made, must be kept." "While I remain in my present position, I shall not attempt to retract or modify the Emancipation Proclamation, nor shall I return to slavery any person who is free by the terms of that Proclamation, or by any of the acts of Congress." And again, "If the people," he says, "by whatever mode or means, should make it an executive duty" to reverse the action of that proclamation, "another, and not I, must be their instrument to perform it." Here speaks the stern stuff from which strong men are made and martyrs come. But the people will stand by the Proclamation; nor will they choose any other hand than his that had written it, to execute it. Not to another can the true champion's glory be given before the field is wholly won.

And now, with clearer vision, and more entire surrender to the divine purpose of events, he consecrates himself to the remaining tasks before him. Henceforth Union and Freedom are synonymous. Two conditions are necessary to peace,— the abolition of all acts of secession, the acceptance of emancipation. But hear again the lofty strains of the chorus, pronouncing judgment on the new aspect of affairs:

"Peace does not appear so distant as it did. I hope it will come soon and come to stay; and so come as to be worth the keeping in all future time. It will then have been proved that among freemen there can be no successful appeal from the ballot to the bullet, and that they who take such appeal are sure to lose their case and pay the cost. And there will be some black men who can remember that with silent tongue, and clinched teeth, and steady eye, and well-poised bayonet, they have helped mankind on to this great consummation, while I fear there will be some white ones unable to forget that with malignant heart and deceitful speech they have striven to hinder it. Still, let us not be over-sanguine of a speedy, final triumph. Let us be quite sober. Let us diligently apply the means, never doubting that a just God, in his own good time, will give us the rightful result."

And so, with ever broader comprehension of the divine meaning of the contest and deeper conviction of the divine hand controlling it, the President renews his vows, and leads on the loyal hosts of freedom to new achievements. Under God, and the providential choice of the nation, he is the instrument for establishing the government on the true democratic basis of liberty, justice, and equality; and so for fulfilling, at last, the prophecy of the Declaration of Independence to all the people of the land.

At Gettysburg, standing among the graves of the heroes, who on that glorious field had given their bodies to death, but who, with their blood, had written their names in the book of immortal life, he opens his address with these memorable sentences: "Four score and seven years ago our fathers brought forth upon this continent a new nation, conceived in liberty and dedicated to the proposition that all men are created equal. Now we are engaged in a great civil war, testing whether that nation, or any nation so conceived and so dedicated, can long endure." And then he solemnly consecrates himself and the nation to finish the work which the heroes there buried had so nobly died for, in order "that this nation, under God, shall have a new birth of freedom, and that government of the people, by the people, and for the people, shall not perish from the earth."

What a perfect recognition of the eternal principles involved in the conflict, and of the Providence watching over and directing with far reaching vision the struggle, does this reverent dedication disclose! Henceforth the nation's President is God's servant; and the war is a religious war,—a religious war more really than if it were to set up some idol of theology, or to enthrone some ecclesiastic power, or to rescue the tomb of Jesus from the hand of unbelieving Saracens: for it is a war to disenthrall and redeem humanity; to rescue a whole continent from being the grave of liberty to become its throne; to lift from the shoulders of a whole people, through the expiatory suffering of just retribution, the monstrous burden of a gigantic iniquity; and to bring, through the reconciliation of obedience to divine law, the grandest opportunity for national and individual development that was ever offered to the human race : it is a war, conducted by unseen powers in the heavens, for the divine right of mankind, without reference to race or class or color, to self-government and self-development,—and the President acknowledges himself but a willing instrument in the hands of the mighty celestial forces directing the combat. Hear how the lips of the loyal leader give utterance to the sentiment of this advanced position : "Now, at the end of three years' struggle, the nation's condition is not what either party, or any man, devised or expected. God alone can claim it. Whither it is tending seems plain. If God now wills the removal of a great wrong, and wills also that we of the North, as well as you of the South, shall pay fairly for our complicity in that wrong, impartial history will find therein new causes to attest and revere the justice and goodness of God."

From this high position it is but a step to the final consummation of the moral progress of the drama. After a political struggle, filled with critical and perilous incidents, and the most solemnly momentous of any that has occurred in our history, the people rechoose for their leader the man who now confesses himself to be, not only the servant of the people, but the servant of God; and they choose him with the express purpose that he may finish the work for republican freedom which the retributive justice of Almighty God has given to his hands. And now the recognition of this truth of the expiatory nature of the war, and the divine

instrumentality of his office culminates in the majestic, almost
awful solemnity of the second Inaugural Address,—which
rises clear above all earthly taint, and human infirmity and
reservation, to the prophetic and divine stand-point. The
political orator is clothed with the mantle of the inspired
prophet; the wise statesman utters his counsels as from the
tribunal of heaven; the leader of the nation becomes the
oracle of divine laws and judgments. From the mouth of
what other human magistrate in all history, shall we find
such utterances as these?   •

  "The Almighty has his own purposes. 'Woe came into
the world because of offences, for it must needs be that
offences come, but woe to that man by whom the offence
cometh.' If we shall suppose that American slavery is one
of these offences, which in the providence of God must needs
come, but which, having continued through his appointed
time, he now wills to remove, and that he gives to both
North and South this terrible war as the woe due to those
by whom the offence came, shall we discern that there is any
departure from those divine attributes which the believers
in a living God always ascribe to him? Fondly do we
hope, fervently do we pray, that this mighty scourge of war
may speedily pass away. Yet if God wills that it continue
until all the wealth piled by the bondman's two hundred
and fifty years of unrequited toil shall be sunk, and until
every drop of blood drawn by the lash shall be paid by
another drawn with the sword,—as was said three thousand
years ago, so still it must be said, that, the 'judgments of the
Lord are true and righteous altogether.' With malice
toward none, with charity for all, with firmness in the right,
as God gives us to see the right, let us strive on to finish
the work we are in, to bind up the nation's wounds, to care
for him who shall have borne the battle, and for his widow

and his orphans, — to do all which may achieve and cherish a just and lasting peace among ourselves and with all nations."

In these words the highest possible utterance of the struggle is reached: the moral triumph of the drama is here achieved; the eternal majesty of the divine laws is acknowledged and vindicated; and the hero stands perfectly submissive to the divine purpose, — docile to the slightest behest of Almighty power, and his eye anointed with heavenly wisdom. These sentences read like a solemn choral response to the half-illuminated, oracularly uttered judgment of the first Inaugural: it is the genius of the Republic, gathering up, as in the ancient chorus, the whole meaning and purpose of the drama, and echoing back, through all the vast, intervening events of the action, the august announcement, that the mystery is unravelled, the struggle ended, the judgment finished and unalterably given. Battles, victories, capitulations, the surrender of armies and towns, the submission of the whole rebellion to the cause that is thus decided for by the celestial umpires, follow in rapid and natural course.

But is the hero to have no more visible triumph than this? Yes; he enters the fallen capital of rebellion and slavery. His entrance into Richmond, with no imperial pomp, with no military escort even, attended only by a few sailors from the navy — emblem of republican Executive simplicity; walking up the long, desolate streets of the captured city, in plain citizen's dress, holding his little boy by the hand — emblem of republican domestic simplicity; followed by a growing throng, as the news ran from street to street, of men, women, and children, from whose limbs his hands had broken the shackles of slavery, — their skin black, but hearts white with joyous gratitude, as they crowded round to hail their deliverer,—baring their heads in reverence before him, and he with instinctive courtesy standing with uncovered head in response—emblem of democratic liberty and equality;—this journey is his triumphal procession; this throng of emancipated slaves, his imperial escort; the benedictions of these new-made freemen are his crown,—the crown of democratic sovereignty.

There is now but one remaining glory that can be accorded. The strict laws of tragedy require that the hero shall die for the truth he has lived for—shall fall in the hour of triumph. And so the President must fall. Does Providence therefore direct the assassin's blow? By no means: only as the providential laws surround, limit, and penetrate every contest between good and evil. But the deadly blow is aimed by the hand of the foe. It is the last, desperate, maddened effort of the struggling combatant. It is the crowning wickedness of the rebellion and slavery. The evil principle of the drama must culminate as well as the good,—it must develop all its inherent and hidden horrors of evil; it must leave no seed of crime that belongs to itself unfruitful; it must leave not the smallest vestige of honor attached to its name. And so, filled with revenge, mad with defeat, inspired with demoniac frenzy, it puts forth all the remaining energy of its mortal strength to slay the man whom it recognizes as the incarnation of all the principles that have contended against it, and the leader of the hosts that have defeated it in battle. It slays him; and thereby, according to the moral intent of the drama, brands itself with everlasting infamy, while it lifts him to an immortal glory, and saves forever the truth to which his life was devoted. The assassin's crime is the rebellion's infamy, and his and freedom's apotheosis. The President falls. But over his grave the nation has a new birth — a resurrection. He seals his testament with his blood, and sanctifies republican truth forever. The President falls. But over his grave his spirit rises into the renowned halls of the celestial heroes, welcomed amid the triumphant songs of a nation redeemed, a people emancipated, a country saved.

With the hero's triumphant departure from earth the drama is ended; but the Spirit of the drama lingers, and utters an epilogue for the awe-struck, listening spectators; and this is the epilogue it speaks:

The President falls: for "where a testament is, there must also of necessity be the death of the testator." The President falls. But his testament remains with us: for a testament is of force after men are dead." The testament remains. The nation, humanity, the world, are its legatees; but we, the people of this generation, are its executors: and we have given sacred bonds, written and attested on many a battle-field with our kindred's blood, that we will administer it, — administer it with exact and impartial justice to all classes and castes and races among us, — in order " that government of the people, by the people, and for the people, shall not perish from the earth."

June 4, 1865.

www.ingramcontent.com/pod-product-compliance
Lightning Source LLC
Chambersburg PA
CBHW021520090426
42739CB00007B/698